Beanbag Bonanza

Accessories, crafts, and games you can make for your beanbag friends!

by
Shari Ann Pence

illustrated by **Jenny Gifford**

Troll

Table of Contents

*This book is dedicated
to children everywhere
who collect beanbag critters
for the FUN of it*

Introduction

This book is filled with fun ways for you to enjoy your beanbag buddies. You can make your own beanbag accessories and furniture. Add flair to your gift giving. Invite your friends to a teddy beanbag tea or other fancy party and play games galore. You'll strike it rich with this gold mine of beanbag fun.

SAFETY TIPS FOR CRAFTS AND PROJECTS

Most of these simple and easy-to-do projects can be done on your own. When, however, you see this symbol 🛑, please be sure to have an adult assist you.

Always use safety scissors when cutting paper and materials. If these are not sharp enough to complete a certain project, ask an adult to help you with the cutting. Never use a hot-glue gun without an adult. Be sure to clean up your work area completely and not to leave any tools or items where young children and pets can get them. Buy craft supplies that are safe and nontoxic. Always read the labels and instructions before you begin.

STEPS TO A GREAT START . . .

1. Make sure an adult is available to assist you should you require help.
2. Read the directions for each project carefully before you begin, and follow them closely for the best results.
3. Choose an area that is safe, spacious, and comfortable.
4. Wear old clothes or a smock when working with glue and paints.

. . . AND A GREAT FINISH

1. Always clean up immediately after you finish a project.
2. Rinse paintbrushes and close paints tightly.
3. Put away scissors, needles, and the hot-glue gun.
4. Store your leftover craft materials in a sealed box.

Easy Accessories

Although your favorite store may sell beanbag accessories, there are many extras you can make yourself. Most of these fun and affordable projects can be created with items you already have in your home. If you need to purchase supplies, go to a craft shop or look for them at a discount store. You'll discover how inexpensive it can be to make your own beanbag accessories.

CRITTER COLLAR AND LEASH

You'll be walking on air with a collar and leash beyond compare!

Supplies:
1 package of black braided elastic,
  ½ inch (1.3 cm) wide
1 package of braided elastic ponytail rings
  (thin, rubber-band width)
2 small split key rings
self-stick Velcro®
needle and thread
beads or appliqués
scissors

How to make:
Collar: Cut a 6- to 7-inch (15- to 18-cm) length of the ½-inch (1.3-cm) braided elastic. Put a small square of the self-stick Velcro® on each end. Secure the Velcro® with a few stitches. Decorate the elastic with appliqués or beads.

Leash: Begin with split key ring #1. Slip one ponytail ring through the key ring and fold over to make two even loops. Hold the loops at the base, by the key ring, and slip another ponytail ring into the opening of the loops (Figure A). Fold over to make even loops again and repeat until all ponytail rings are linked in the chain. To end the chain: Take the last two loops of your chain and slip them into the split of key ring #2, as you would attach a key (Figure B). Loop the collar through key ring #1 and use the Velcro® to fasten it around your critter's neck.

Figure A   Figure B

CHIMING COWBELL

'Til the cows come home, hear a jingle as they roam.

Supplies:
1 package of small cowbells
   (available at craft stores)
1 package of elastic metallic cord
scissors

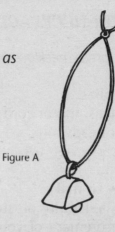

Figure A

How to make:
Cut a 6-inch (15-cm) length of elastic cord. Thread through the ring at the top of the cowbell. Bring the ends of the cord together and tie in a single knot (Figure A).

With several bells in a package and plenty of cord, make one for each of the cows in your barnyard. Give extra cowbells to your friends.

NIFTY NECKLACE

This pretty necklace makes a great gift.

Supplies:
elastic string or cord
craft beads
scissors

How to make:
Cut a length of string a few inches longer than the measurement of your beanbag animal's neck. Tie a large knot at one end of the string. Thread your beads onto the string. When the beads equal the measurement of the animal's neck, bring the ends together and tie them in a knot. Clip off the loose ends of the string.

BEANBAG BOLO

Lasso your favorite friend with a western tie.

Supplies:
1 thin strip of leather or cord
1 large craft gem or
   a flat metal concho
1 drinking straw
tape
scissors

Back   Front

How to make:
Cut two pieces of straw, each ½ inch (1.3 cm) long. Tape the straws to the back of the gem or concho. Slip one end of the leather or cord into each straw to form a loop. Tie a knot in each end of the leather or cord. Slip the bolo over your beanbag animal's head and slide the craft gem or concho toward the neck to tighten.

CHARMING EARRINGS

Charm your critters with these dazzling ear danglers.

Supplies:
thin satin ribbon 10 inches
  (25 cm) long
charms
scissors

How to make:
Cut the ribbon in half. Thread one piece of ribbon through one charm. Tie the ribbon around your beanbag animal's ear, making sure the charm is below the ear. Repeat these steps to make a matching earring for the other ear.

BEAUTIFUL BONNET

Make a straw bonnet for your special pal.

Supplies:

🛑 Ask an adult to assist you.

1 doll-size straw hat
  (available at craft stores)
1 satin rose
thin ribbon
scissors
hot-glue gun

How to make:
Cut an 8-inch (20-cm) length of ribbon. Hot-glue the middle of the ribbon to the front of the hat, and continue to glue the ribbon around the crown of the hat where it meets the brim. Leave a ½-inch (1.3-cm) opening in the back. Tie a bow with the ribbon ends. Glue the satin rose on top of the bow.

CRITTER BOOTIES

Cozy toes are at your fingertips.

Supplies:
1 large knit glove
lace trim
needle and thread
scissors

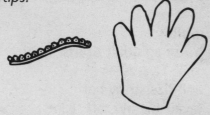

How to make:
Cut the fingers off the glove, allowing at least 2 inches (5 cm) for each bootie. Sew lace trim to the open end of each of the four fingers. Slip the booties onto your beanbag animal. Fold down the lace cuff on each sock for a cozy crew. You can decorate the booties with sequins, buttons, or fabric paint if you wish.

SOCK SWEATER VEST

Make a warm top for your Arctic pals.

Supplies:
1 child-size tube sock
scissors

How to make:
Cut a "V" shape in the middle of the toe of the sock. Make sure it is large enough to fit the animal's head. Start small; you can always cut away more if needed. Slip the sock over your critter's head and mark where the wings or paws will fit. Remove the sock and cut slits in the sides for the sleeve openings. Cut off the bottom of the sock if it is too long for your animal.

Add trim, fabric paints, or buttons to dress up the sweater vest.

CINCHY SCARF

Use your head(wrap) for a smart scarf.

Supplies:

STOP Ask an adult to help you choose a headwrap.

1 cloth headwrap
3 to 4 inches (7.5 to 10 cm) of fringe trim
   (available at craft stores)
needle and thread
scissors

How to make:

Cut through the headwrap at the short seam that joins both ends together. Trim away the seam. Sew the fringe trim onto the cut ends to make a smart scarf.

Add appliqués or paint accents. You can even embroider designs on the scarf.

PETITE PURSE

A handy handbag to hold your beanbag buddy's accessories.

Supplies:
1 felt square, 9 x 12 inches (23 x 30 cm)
1 button
ribbon or cord, 12 inches (30 cm) long
needle and thread
scissors

How to make:
Cut the felt in two sections as shown in the pattern below. Sew the button where the "X" is drawn. Stitch the small piece onto the large piece—but only around the edge, leaving an opening along the top of the small piece. Cut a slit at the top of the large piece as shown. Cut very small slits at the "O"'s. Pull the cord through the "O" slits and knot to form a strap. Fold over the top flap and button to close.

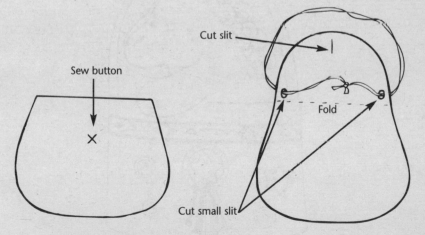

Sew button

Cut slit

Fold

Cut small slit

TERRIFIC TOTE

Tote your favorite pals in a canvas carryall.

Supplies:
1 small plain canvas tote bag
  (available at craft or fabric stores)
fabric paints and stencils
sponges
buttons
ribbons
jewels
appliqués

How to make:
Decorate the tote bag with paints and stencils or sponges.
Optional: Add buttons, ribbons, jewels, and appliqués.

*Check out this great
idea for decorating
a critter carryall!*

COZY BATH WRAP

A warm and fuzzy feeling for your furry friends.

Supplies:
1 washcloth
1 yard (1m) wide satin ribbon
pen or pencil
scissors

How to make:
Figure A—Fold in two sides of the washcloth to meet in the middle of the washcloth.

Figure B—Draw five slits on each edge as shown below, and cut the slits open with scissors. Thread the ribbon through the two slits as shown.

Figure C—Fold the bottom flap up. You will continue to thread the ribbon through each of the matching slits.

Figure D—Thread the ribbon through both pieces of the washcloth in the direction of the arrows as shown.

Figure E—Tighten the stitches as you go along. Tie the ribbon in a bow to finish the bath wrap.

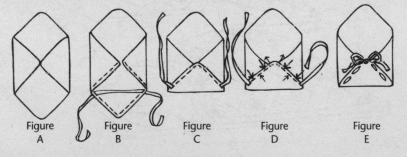

Figure A   Figure B   Figure C   Figure D   Figure E

SLUMBER SACK

Kitchen hot pads will keep your bedtime beanbag friends warm and toasty.

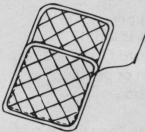

Supplies:
2 hot pads (1 tall, 1 short)
needle and thread
scissors

How to make:
Place the smaller hot pad on top of the larger hot pad, making sure the two sides and bottom of each pad line up. Stitch the bottoms and sides together along the outer edge of the material (not on the seams), leaving the top edge of the small hot pad open. Make sure the top inch on both sides of the hot pads is securely stitched. Slip your beanbag buddies in at the top.

Fine Furnishings

Although most doll furniture would fit your beanbag animals' home-furnishing needs, it can be quite expensive. Why not bring out the creative carpenter inside of you and build furniture yourself? You can design fine furnishings from recyclables, toys, and other household items. It's fun and easy to do!

BEANBAG BED

Dreams are sweeter in a bed built by you.

Supplies:
1 cigar box
1 small kitchen towel
2 small washcloths
needle and thread
polyester fiberfill
  (or cotton balls)
scissors

How to make:
Carefully cut or tear the top flap off the box. Fold the kitchen towel into a square large enough to tuck in as the mattress. Cut one washcloth in half so you have two rectangle shapes. Lay one rectangle on top of the other and sew a running stitch along three edges of the two pieces (Figure A). Turn the material inside out. Stuff and fluff with fiberfill or cotton balls. Stitch the fourth side to close (Figure B). Perch your pint-size pillow on top of the bed. The other washcloth is a warm blanket.

Figure A

Figure B

BANDANNA HAMMOCK

A swinging place to sleep.

Supplies:

🛑 Ask an adult to assist you.

1 bandanna   hot-glue gun
4 ice cream or craft sticks   scissors
heavyweight string

How to make:

Spread the bandanna on a table or other flat surface. Fold the top corner about two-thirds over the bandanna (Figure A). Fold the bottom corner up. Fold the point in and glue the top edge so both edges are the same length (Figure B).

Figure A

Figure B

Measure 6 inches (15 cm) from one end of the bandanna and position a craft stick as shown below. Fold the two sides slightly inward so the bandanna will fit completely underneath the stick. Glue the craft stick onto the top of the folded end of the bandanna. Turn the bandanna over and glue another craft stick directly behind the first. Repeat on the other end.

Tie two 12-inch (30-cm) lengths of string into circles. Fold each tip of the bandanna over one of the circles of string and glue to secure.

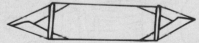

BASIC BLOCK CHAIR

A super seat that really stacks up.

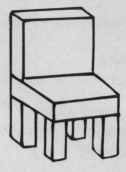

Supplies:
🛑 Ask an adult to assist you.

1 small box of
   wooden toy blocks
hot-glue gun

How to make:
Build the wooden chair by gluing the blocks one to another, as shown. (Remember to ask your parent—or younger sibling!—for permission to glue the blocks.) Refer to the illustration before you begin, and select blocks that are uniform in size. Start by gluing pieces together to form the bottom of the seat. Next, glue pieces to the back of the seat to make the backrest. To finish, glue the legs to the underside of the seat. You can add arms too, if you like. Make sure the glue is set before you invite your beanbag animals to sit.

BEANBAG CHAIR

Plop your pals onto a floppy chair.

Supplies:
1 knit hat (any size)
uncooked rice
needle and thread
scissors

How to make:
Wash and line dry your old (or new) knit hat. Fill the hat three-quarters full with instant rice. Bring the open ends of the hat together and stitch with a needle and thread to close.

SHOE BOX INN

Spacious living with room for guests.

Supplies:
4 large shoe boxes
packaging tape
wallpaper and
  fabric scraps
scissors
glue

How to make:
Stack the shoe boxes as shown in the illustration above. Tape together on all sides (one to another, and then around the outside to secure). Decorate the rooms with clever crafts you can design yourself. Here are a few simple suggestions.

A small sauce container from a take-out restaurant makes a lovely lampshade. For the base, use a tall shampoo cap.

The plastic prop inside a delivery pizza is an end table.

Stack and glue together empty matchboxes to make a dresser.

Frame mini masterpieces with chenille stems (pipe cleaners) to adorn the walls.

Take an old sock and cut off the top ribbing. Cut one line to open the tube, so the material will lay flat. Use the scissors to trim and cut a rug.

Wrap It Up

CLEVER GIFT GIVING AND DRESSY DISPLAY IDEAS

This chapter is filled with fanciful tips for presenting the most memorable presents. Beanbag critters make great birthday gifts, holiday presents, and get-well wishes.

These wonderful ideas can also be used to dress up your room. Showcase your favorite beanbag friends in a special place on your headboard, dresser, or shelf.

PIE TIN POND

This clever pond is as easy as pie to make.

Fill a pie tin with two packages of cat's eyes marbles (available at craft stores). A duck will wade for you, and a frog will leap for joy if you add a felt lily pad.

HABITAT HOUSE

Create a cozy critter haven.

Fill a small plastic creature house (in the pet section of retail stores) or a clear plastic storage container with aquarium rocks, plastic plants, and a branch or log. Move in a lizard, turtle, snake, or spider.

BED IN A BASKET

Shrink a pet bed to fit your beanbag puppy pals.

Use a paper plate as a pattern to cut circles from two felt squares. Place the circles together and stitch along the outer edges of the felt with a running stitch, leaving an opening 3 to 4 inches (7.5 to 10 cm) long. Stuff with polyester fiberfill (available at craft or fabric stores) or cotton balls. Complete the stitching to close. Place the felt pillow in a straw paper-plate holder.

SIDE DISHES

Cats and dogs side by side.

Purchase a small double-sided dog or cat dish. Write your cat's name on one bowl and your dog's name on the other. Decorate with paints and stickers. Place your dog and cat in their dishes. Now give the dog some dry treat bones and the cat a toy. Wrap with clear cellophane and display.

COFFEE BEANS

Present a mug filled with beanbag kisses and hugs.

Discount and dollar stores sell inexpensive coffee mugs. For a grown-up, add sample packs of instant coffee and a coffee stirrer or serve at tea time with flavored tea bags and a huggable critter. For your friends, hot chocolate and a beanbag pal will warm their hearts.

BEANBAG BURRITOS

A tasty treat for your best friend.

Wrap your gift beanbag animal in a material tortilla. Use a bandanna, washcloth, or cloth napkin and fold it like a burrito shell. Save a clean burrito or taco paper wrapper from your favorite fast food place and use as a clever camouflage.

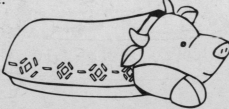

SWEET TOOTH

For someone who's sweet
on beanbag critters.

Save a pretty chocolate box after Valentine's Day, or ask your favorite chocolate connoisseur to empty a box for you. Surround the animal with sweet treats and wrap the box. Tell your friends there's no need to worry, this treat is mostly sugar free.

SURPRISE BON BONS

I scream, you scream, we all scream for ice cream . . . and
beanbag pals!

Rinse and dry a one-gallon ice cream container. Whatever the flavor is on the package, wrap the animal in tissue paper to match. For example, draw chocolate chunks with a marking pen on white tissue for chocolate chip. Wrap in pink tissue for strawberry. Since you'll *have* to eat the ice cream first, pick your favorite flavor.

33

RAINBOW SEASHELL

A colorful home for deep-sea creatures.

A sandwich-sized white take-out container from a restaurant is a critter-sized seashell. For a rainbow seashell, decorate with colored tissue paper. Tear the tissue into small pieces. Dip a damp sponge brush into white glue and paint an area on top of the shell. Attach pieces of colored tissue while the glue is wet. Smooth wrinkles with your fingers. Allow plenty of time for your seashell to dry.

BEACH PAIL

A bucket full of beach-time fun.

Beach pails are seasonal, so pick up a few extras during the summer clearance sales. Fill the bottom of the pail with shredded tan (sand-colored) paper. Add a few seashells, a sample size of sunscreen, sunglasses, and your favorite ocean beanbag pal.

TREASURE CHEST

Keep a favorite critter in this cool treasure chest.

Turn a small shoe box into a treasure chest. Cover the box with brown construction paper. Make a hinge on one side by running a length of packaging tape across the edge of the lid where it meets the box. Draw chest details on the box with a black marking pen. Fill the treasure chest with costume jewelry (from swap meets and yard sales), a map drawn on a torn, crumpled piece of brown grocery bag, and a favorite island friend.

BOWL-A-RAMA

A diorama in the deep blue sea.

Purchase a goldfish bowl at a discount store. Lay the bowl on its side, on top of a plain piece of paper, and trace the outline. Cut out the shape and decorate the paper with scenes from the ocean. Put the scene into the bowl and tape it to one side, facing in. Fill the bottom of the bowl with shredded blue tissue paper and add a deep-sea diving beanbag pal.

BACK-TO-SCHOOL SUPPLIES

A great gift that really makes the grade.

Fill a cigar box with back-to-school supplies (pencils, crayons, glue, ruler, notepad) and your favorite critter. It all adds up to a great gift!

GREEN THUMB

A great gardening gift for your plant-loving friends.

Decorate an inexpensive plastic clay-colored pot with paint. Plant a beanbag animal in the middle and heap on the gardening gifts: some seed packets, canvas gloves, and a plastic garden shovel. Make pretty plant sticks with craft sticks and some markers.

Let's Party!

Although birthdays are a very special reason to host a party, why not celebrate every day? There are many events that deserve recognition. Did you get an A on a test? Did you meet a new friend? Whether it's Groundhog Day or your beanbag buddy's birthday, there's always a good reason to celebrate!

BARN DANCE

Invite your friends to a barnyard ball.

Decorations:

- A small loaf pan for a feeding trough
- Wood shavings (or small-animal bedding) spread in a large, flat box for the dance floor
- Bandannas for tablecloths or picnic blankets

Activities:

Play "Needle in a Haystack," also known as hide-and-seek, with a straw. Take turns hiding and seeking a drinking straw.

Play "Mending Fences." Stack wooden blocks to see who can build the tallest fence.

Favors:

Treat your beanbag pals and your human friends to a pail of feed. Take a bathroom-size paper drinking cup and half of a chenille stem (pipe cleaner). Poke two holes directly across from each other near the top of the cup. Bend the chenille stem to make a handle and slip the ends into the holes. Twist to secure. Make one for each guest.

Fill the pails with homemade trail mix (pretzel sticks, small crackers, raisins, cereal, chocolate candies, dried fruit).

PET SHOW

Parade your pets in an event to showcase their best.

Decorations:
- Red, white, and blue paper streamers
- Shoe boxes covered in pretty paper for the podiums
- Red felt squares placed in a row for a royal red carpet runway

Activities:
Judge the beanbag entrants and be sure to award each participant with a blue ribbon. Here are some prize-winning ideas: Nicest coat, most well groomed, prettiest collar, most obedient, best of show. Create one category per entry. See "Favors" for easy-to-make award ribbons.

Play "Give the Dog a Bone." Toss bone-shaped treat biscuits into a dog dish (or any dish).

Favors:
Wrap leftover treat biscuits from the "Give the Dog a Bone" game (or some human cookies) in small plastic bags and tie with a ribbon.

Press a paper muffin baking cup flat onto a kitchen counter. Glue the ends of two pieces of a wide blue ribbon to the middle of the muffin cup. Center and glue a frozen juice lid on top of the ribbon and to the muffin cup to make a prize-winning award ribbon.

TEDDY BEAR TEA

It's tea for two, three, four—or maybe more.

Decorations:
- A vase of fresh, or silk, flowers in the center of the table
- Party favor rings make perfect little napkin rings
- A play tea set on the teatime table

Activities:
Play "Tea Bag Hopscotch." Use a tea bag with a coin taped to the paper as a hopscotch marker.

Play "Crumpet Croquet." Make a crumpet by crumpling a piece of gift wrapping tissue into a ball. Use a wooden spoon as a mallet. For the croquet wires, use chenille stems (pipe cleaners). Shape and tape the stems to the carpet with masking tape or poke into the lawn. (Ask an adult before putting masking tape on the carpet.)

Favors:
Roll two hard-candy sticks in a small paper doily and tie with a ribbon.

Make a personalized placecard for each guest. Fold an index card in half. Write each guest's name on a card. Tape a small square of stickers on the back so your guests can decorate their place cards.

SEASIDE CELEBRATION
Declare your devotion with a party by the ocean.

Decorations:
- Beach balls and sand toys
- Beach towels for table covers and picnic blankets
- Plastic pails filled with sea-animal beanbag pals

Activities:

Play "Beanbags in the Sand." Fill a tinfoil baking pan with sand. Take turns drawing pictures of your favorite beanbag critters in the sand (use your fingertip or the end of an unsharpened pencil). The first one to guess correctly takes the next turn.

Play "Buried Treasure." After playing the drawing game, bury trinkets in the sand while your guests hide their eyes. Let them take turns digging for buried treasure. Make sure each guest finds an equal share of the loot.

Favors:

"Seashells on the Seashore." Cut 10-inch (25-cm) squares from sandpaper, one for each guest. Give each guest a few seashells, two cotton balls, plant stems, blue paint, and brushes. Provide a bottle of glue for your guests to design their own seashore. Paint a corner of the sandpaper blue for the water. Pull apart cotton balls and shape into sea foam. Add the seashells and plant stems for seaweed.

Make a paper-cup pail (see instructions on page 38) and fill with fish-shaped crackers.

SOCK HOP

This beanbag party is a blast from the past!

Decorations:
- Tie helium-filled balloons to a six-pack of soda bottles.
- Buy fuzzy dice or make giant dice with gift boxes (draw dots on each of the box's six sides).
- Make records with black and colored construction paper. Write hit song titles on the records.

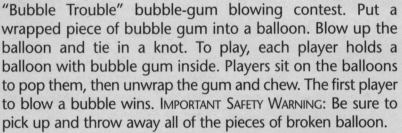

Activities:
"Bubble Trouble" bubble-gum blowing contest. Put a wrapped piece of bubble gum into a balloon. Blow up the balloon and tie in a knot. To play, each player holds a balloon with bubble gum inside. Players sit on the balloons to pop them, then unwrap the gum and chew. The first player to blow a bubble wins. IMPORTANT SAFETY WARNING: Be sure to pick up and throw away all of the pieces of broken balloon.

Play "Penny Loafers." Pick a beanbag pal's birth year and find a penny with that date. Add other pennies with different dates. Ask each guest to put one of the pennies in his or her shoe. Dance to a fifties tune, then announce the winning year. Ask the dancers to check the pennies in their shoes. Award a prize to the person whose penny has the winning beanbag birth year.

Favors:
Plastic bracelets for your beanbag pals to hula in a hoop.

Ask your grandparents which candies were popular in the fifties. Buy and give these "penny" candies to your guests.

BIG TOP CIRCUS

Clown around with carnival games.

Decorations:
- Red and white balloons and streamers
- Circus beanbag critters (elephant, lion, tiger, seal, horse)
- A circus train made with cardboard boxes

Activities:
Set up a midway of carnival games, such as:

Dime Toss. Toss dimes to land on plates and in mugs.

Fish Bowl. Bounce a Ping-Pong ball into a fish bowl.

Milk Carton Toss. Knock down empty paper milk cartons with rolled-up sock balls.

Three-Ring Circus. Set up three round baskets and toss a different stuffed animal into each ring.

Ring Toss. Toss plastic bracelets around the necks of soda bottles.

Favors:
Animal crackers, plastic circus animals, peanuts, and cotton candy

BEANBAG BIRTHDAY

Throw a party that's a piece of cake.

Decorations:
- Save partyware and gift wrap from your own parties.
- Ask an adult to help you make a cake or cupcakes.
- Tie ribbons around small bags of jelly beans.

Activities:
Pin-the-Tail on the Beanbag. Draw the birthday critter on a piece of posterboard, without its tail. Cut out tails from construction paper and add a piece of tape to each tail. Blindfold each player in turn and spin him or her around. The object of the game is for the blindfolded player to stick the tail as close to the actual spot on the animal as possible.

Beanbag Toss. Toss beanbag animals at a target.

Bean Counters. Guess how many jelly beans are in a jar.

Jumping Beans. Toss dried beans into a garden pot. The winner is the one who "plants" the most jumping beans.

Favors:
Make a pint-sized party hat. Trim a regular-sized paper party hat, leaving approximately 2 inches (5 cm) at the top. Add a ruffle trim to the bottom and glue a pom pom to the top. Trim and tape elastic string to the bottom of the hat for a perfect fit.

Make mini-bookmarks. Cut a blank index card lengthwise, then design a bookmark featuring your birthday critter.

Happy Holidays

Celebrate the holidays with these fun activities, crafts, and gifts for your favorite beanbag pals and human friends.

VALENTINE'S DAY

Give a gift from your heart for Valentine's Day.

Supplies:
2 pieces of red felt, 9 x 12 inches (23 x 30.5 cm)
needle and thread
fabric paints
appliqués, beads, buttons,
  or gems
scissors

How to make:
Draw a heart shape on a piece of paper, large enough to cover the entire piece of felt. Cut the paper pattern out, trace onto the two pieces of felt, and cut out the felt hearts. Lay the hearts one of top of the other. With the needle and thread, stitch around the outside edge of the hearts, leaving the top open. Decorate the felt heart with fabric paints, appliqués, beads, buttons, or gems. Fill your heart with a special beanbag buddy.

ST. PATRICK'S DAY

Bestow the luck of the Irish on your beanbag friends.

Supplies:
green construction paper
posterboard
aluminum foil
1 shiny penny
small gift bag
scissors

How to make:
Cut a four-leaf clover from the
construction paper for good-luck
charm #1.

Cut a horseshoe from the
posterboard and cover with
aluminum foil for good-luck
charm #2.

Add a shiny penny for good-
luck charm #3.

Put all of your good-luck charms
in a mini-gift bag and give
to one lucky critter.

EASTER

A tisket, a tasket, a handy little basket.

Supplies:
a miniature craft basket (available at craft stores)
holiday grass
jelly beans
marking pens

How to make:
Line the miniature basket with holiday grass. Draw designs on the jelly beans with marking pens to make miniature "Easter eggs." Fill the basket with the "eggs." IMPORTANT SAFETY WARNING: Do not eat jelly beans that you have decorated.

Plan an egg hunt for your beanbag friends.

FOURTH OF JULY

A super-safe fireworks display.

Supplies:
empty toilet-tissue rolls
gift-wrap tissue
yarn or ribbon
wrapped candies or confetti streamers
scissors

How to make:
Fill each toilet-tissue roll with wrapped candies or confetti streamers. Wrap the roll in a piece of tissue paper, leaving about 3 inches (7 cm) of tissue paper on each side. Twist the tissue ends and tie with yarn or ribbon.

These fun-filled firecrackers make great gifts! Hide a mini-beanbag inside for a spectacular surprise.

HALLOWEEN

Dress all your critters in fun Halloween costumes!

Supplies:
beanbag animal and doll accessories
fabric or felt squares
needle and thread

How to make:
Look at the illustrations below for some fun costume ideas.
Then ask an adult to help you sew the felt or fabric to make
these costumes.

Host a Halloween party for your friends with a create-a-
critter costume contest. Award trick-or-treat prizes to
everyone.

THANKSGIVING

A Plymouth "pet" rock.

Supplies:
1 smooth stone
various colored paints
1 paintbrush
1 permanent marking pen

How to make:
Design a pet rock paperweight portraying your favorite beanbag animal. Express your thanks to a special friend by presenting him or her with a Plymouth "pet" rock.

On the back of the rock, write a message of friendship and thanks. Here are some ideas:

"It's smooth sailing with a friend like you."
"I thank my lucky stars for a friend like you."
"Our friendship is rock solid."

CHRISTMAS/HANUKKAH

Deck the halls—and walls—with these holiday wreaths.

Supplies:
pictures of beanbag animals
   from a magazine
paper plate
holiday trims
crayons
soda-pop top
glue
tape
scissors

How to make:
Cut the middle out of the paper plate to make a wreath. Color the wreath in festive holiday colors. Glue pictures of beanbag animals to the wreath. Add holiday trims, such as fabrics, beads, buttons, tiny pine cones, berries, ribbons, and so forth. Tape the soda-pop top to the back of the plate for a hanger.

One magazine should provide enough pictures to make several wreaths. Give as gifts to your friends to greet the season.

Critter Toys

You would be surprised to learn how many toys and accessories you can find for your beanbag animals at a discount store. All it takes is a lot of imagination and just a little allowance.

These ideas will help you discover where to look to find fun toys and accessories for your beanbag pals.

SPORTS GEAR

Yell and cheer for this neat sports gear.

Convert a coin purse into a mini sport bag. Look for the styles that resemble a miniature duffel or tote bag.

Sports Equipment:
Terry cloth ponytail rings make good "no sweat" headbands.

Color white Ping-Pong balls with marking pens to make a selection of sports balls (soccer, basketball, baseball).

Make a hockey stick from ice cream or craft sticks. Use a small candy-coated tart for a puck.

An ice cream or craft stick can also be used for a tennis racket handle. Buy a piece of white plastic canvas (less than 50¢ in most discount-store craft departments) to use for the strings. Cut the plastic canvas in an oval shape and frame the outside edge with colored tape. Glue the frame and strings (head of the racket) onto a craft stick. Wrap the bottom of the handle in colored tape. Use a yellow gumball for the tennis ball.

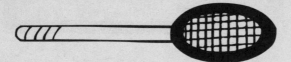

A golf ball is a critter-sized bowling ball. For the pins use skinny wooden blocks.

JUST FOR FUN

Read to your beanbag pals:
Tiny books are available
anywhere books are sold.

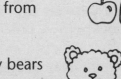

Miniature erasers become play food and toys.
Serve play food on a platter made from
a frozen-juice lid.

Look for miniature dolls and teddy bears
in discount, party, and craft stores.

Many famous brand-name toys have been modeled into
keychains. In fact, a lot of fun accessories can be found on
the end of a key ring. In addition to toys, look for miniature
phones, cameras, sports equipment, flashlights, crayons,
and more. Look in discount and dollar stores for ideas.

Specialty candy and gift shops
sell miniature gumball machines.

Miniature tool sets.

Make a jumprope from a shoelace. Cut to the correct size
and wind colored tape around the ends to make handles.

Many party favors come in
small sizes: yo-yos, tops, jacks,
kaleidoscopes, boats,
pocket pinballs, and
maze puzzles.

ACCESSORIES

Check out these sources for great accessories!

Doll Accessories:
bonnets
cowboy hats
doll glasses
doll shoes
parasols

Crafts:
small watering cans
miniature garden tools
yarn (make yarn balls for cats)
seashells
wicker chairs
tiny baskets

Wedding, Shower, and Party Favors:
plastic cups and mugs
baby bottles
tiny clothes pins
mini-paint sets, puzzles, jewelry, toys, and games

Miniatures:
This department of a craft or discount store will have many small surprises for you to share with your beanbag friends.

Games Galore

If your critters are collecting dust bunnies on the shelf, invite them to join in these fun games.

CRITTER COUNTING

Put all of your beanbag friends in one basket.

Take an inventory of your beanbag animals to see how many you have. Count them in categories: how many cats, how many dogs, how many ocean animals, and so forth. Count them in colors: how many black animals, how many white animals, how many striped animals, and so forth.

HOOP SHOTS

Practice your ring-toss skills.

Cut the middle from a large butter-tub lid, leaving only the outer ring. Tape a length of yarn (leave a tail) to the inside of the ring and wrap the yarn around the entire ring to smooth the edge. When you reach the tail again, tie the two ends together and secure with a knot.

Put a few of your beanbag critters across the room or on a table. Throw the hoop from across the room to ring an animal. Play with a friend or two on a rainy day.

TIC-TAC-TOE

Here's a fun way to get three in a row.

Draw a tic-tac-toe grid on a large piece of posterboard. Instead of X's, one player uses cat beanbags. In place of O's, the other player uses dog beanbags. Play just like tic-tac-toe, only with cats and dogs! Save the posterboard to play again.

BEANBAG BOARD GAME

Master a monopoly on fun.

Design your own board game! Use the pattern below to set up a game on a large piece of posterboard. Be sure to make the spaces big enough to include the written instructions for each square. Borrow one die from another board game to play. Use beanbag critters for the game pieces.

Here are some examples of what to write in the spaces:
• You're bored. Go back 2 spaces.
• Mud puddle. Go back to Start.
• You helped a cat out of a tree. Go forward 3 spaces.
• Nap time. Skip 1 turn.

Now it's your turn to think of ideas to add to the game.

Decorate the board with trees, flowers, a pond, and more.

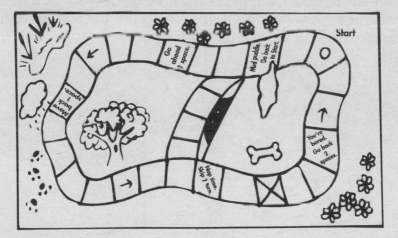

A DAY AT THE RACES

A winner's circle of fast-paced races.

You will need a large piece of posterboard or a length of brown butcher paper. For each beanbag critter in the race, you will need to draw a row of 10 to 12 race markers. For a horse race, draw horseshoes. For a frog-leaping race, draw lily pads. For tortoises and hares, draw carrots. For a swim meet with ocean animals, draw clams.

To play, each critter will start at the edge of the board. Roll one die to determine the number of spaces your beanbag will move forward. Take turns rolling the die and moving until an animal reaches the finish line.

Beanbag Bungalows

Storing your beanbag collection might present a problem. If your room is bursting at the seams because you have too many friends, here are several simple solutions:

FEET FIRST
An over-the-door hanging shoe rack is perfect for holding up to 25 beanbag animals. Look for these see-through shoe files at discount stores.

BOTTLE BOXES
Ask a retailer who sells bottles or glasses to rescue a box of dividers from the recycle bin. Paint the box or cover it with paper for beanbag apartment compartments.

TISSUE-BOX TOWERS
A high-rise of cube-shaped tissue boxes makes cozy condos. Stack with openings facing front in rows of 3 x 3 or 4 x 4. Tape one to another, then secure with tape around the outside.

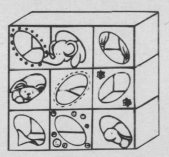